F☉CUS ON
Comprehension
Introductory

Louis Fidge

Stories with familiar settings	Traditional stories	Stories from other cultures	Stories with predictable or patterned language	Stories by significant children's authors	Texts with language play	Poems with familiar settings	Poems from other cultures	Poems with predictable or patterned language	Poems by significant children's poets	Poems with language play	Instructions/directions	Alphabetically ordered texts	Explanations	Information texts	Reports
FICTION											**NON-FICTION**				
✓			✓												
					✓		✓	✓							
											✓			✓	
					✓		✓								
											✓			✓	
					✓	✓									
✓			✓												
	✓														
													✓	✓	
					✓			✓							
		✓													
											✓	✓	✓		
	✓	✓													
												✓	✓		
✓		✓	✓												
✓			✓												
					✓		✓		✓						
												✓	✓	✓	
												✓	✓		
			✓												
					✓	✓	✓								
✓		✓													

Contents

UNIT 1 Alfie's Feet

Think ahead

Do you like getting a new pair of shoes? Why?

When they got in, Alfie sat down at once and unwrapped his new boots. He put them on all by himself and walked about in them, stamp! stamp! stamp! He went into the kitchen to show Mum and Dad and Annie Rose, stamping his feet all the way, stamp! stamp! stamp! The boots were very smart and shiny but they felt funny.

Alfie wanted to go out again right away. So he put on his mac, and Dad took his book and his newspaper and they went off to the park.

Alfie stamped in a lot of mud and walked through a lot of puddles, splish, splash, SPLOSH! He frightened some sparrows who were having a bath. He even frightened two big ducks. They went hurrying back to their pond, walking with their feet turned in.

Alfie looked down at his feet. They still felt funny. They kept turning outwards. Dad was sitting on a bench. They both looked at Alfie's feet. Suddenly Alfie knew what was wrong!

From *Alfie's Feet* by Shirley Hughes

➡️ *Thinking back*

Finish each sentence with the correct answer.
1 Alfie had some new
  a) books   b) stamps   c) boots
2 Alfie went out with
  a) Mum   b) Dad   c) Annie Rose
3 Alfie went to
  a) the park   b) the shops   c) school
4 Alfie walked in
  a) the river   b) the snow   c) the mud

➡️ *Thinking about it*

Write a sentence to answer each question.
1 What were Alfie's boots like?
2 Why did Alfie wear a mac when he went out?
3 Why did the ducks hurry back to their pond?
4 What do you think was wrong with Alfie's boots?

➡️ *Thinking it through*

1 Write down how you think Alfie felt about his boots.
2 What noise did Alfie make with his boots
  a) in the kitchen?   b) in the puddles?
3 Write the noise these animals make
  a) birds b) ducks c) dogs d) lions
4 Write about some shoes you would really like.

UNIT 2 Mice

Think ahead

What do you think of mice? Are they nice or nasty?
Why?

I think mice
Are rather nice.

    Their tails are long,
    Their faces small,
    They haven't any chins at all.
    Their ears are pink,
    Their teeth are white,
    They run about
    The house at night.
    They nibble things they shouldn't touch
    And no one seems
    To like them much.

But I think mice
Are nice.

From *Mice* by Rose Fyleman

Thinking back

Write if each sentence is true or false.

1 The person who wrote the poem thinks mice are nice.
2 Mice have large faces.
3 Mice have green ears.
4 Mice nibble things.

Thinking about it

1 There are lots of facts about mice in the poem. Make them into a Mouse Fact File. Add any other things you know about mice. Do it like this:

Mouse Fact File
Mice have long tails and small faces.

Thinking it through

Think of some good answers for these questions.

1 Write the word in the poem that rhymes with:
   a) mice   b) small   c) white   d) touch
2 Give some reasons why some people may not like mice.
3 List some other animals that come out at night.
4 Find out what the word 'nocturnal' means.

UNIT 3 The Car Ride

Think ahead

Imagine you went out for a car ride in the countryside. What sort of things might you see?

Offley Village

Bluebell Wood

church

pond

windmill

Webb's Farm

Riverside Restaurant

bridge

river

8

➡ *Thinking back*

Write a sentence to answer each question.
1 What village do you pass through?
2 What is the name of the wood?
3 Is the windmill in the village or on the farm?
4 Is the pond near the village or the bridge?

➡ *Thinking about it*

These sentences tell of the things you saw on your car ride, but they are muddled up. Write them again in the correct order.
- Outside the village we passed a pond.
- After we turned the first corner there was a farm.
- First we drove through Offley village and saw the church.
- Soon we went across a bridge over a river.
- Near the pond we saw Bluebell Wood.

➡ *Thinking it through*

1 Imagine you stopped to have a look around the village. Describe some of the things you might have seen.
2 Name a good place to stop for a picnic on your car ride. Say why.
3 Pretend you carried on with your journey. Write three more sentences about some other things you might have passed.

UNIT 4 Nursery Rhymes Old and New

Think ahead
What nursery rhymes do you know?

Little Jack Horner
Sat in the corner
Eating his Christmas pie.
He put in his thumb
And pulled out a plum
And said, 'What a good boy am I!'

Traditional Nursery Rhyme

Little Sue Horner
Sneaks round the corner
Munching salt crisps on the sly.
She won't eat her lunch
If she takes one more crunch
And her mum's baked a nice liver pie.

From *Little Sue Horner* by Lucy Coats

Choose the best ending for each sentence.

1 Little Jack Horner _____.
   a) slept in the corner   b) sat in the corner
2 Little Sue Horner was eating _____.
   a) crisps   b) Christmas pie
3 Little Jack Horner put in his thumb and pulled out _____.
   a) a sum   b) a plum
4 Little Sue Horner's mum baked _____.
   a) an apple pie   b) a liver pie

Thinking about it

Write a sensible sentence to answer each question.

1 Which is a boy and which is a girl?
2 Why did Jack think he was good?
3 Why do you think Sue sneaked round the corner?
4 Do you think Sue was naughty? Why?
5 What do you think Sue's mum will say to her when she can't eat her dinner?

Thinking it through

1 Which do you think is the oldest nursery rhyme? Why?
2 Which rhyme do you prefer? Give your reasons.
3 Write another nursery rhyme you know.

UNIT 5　Making a Peanut Butter and Jam Sandwich

Think ahead

Why do we need to read instructions carefully?

You need:

bread

knife

peanut butter

jam

What to do:

1 Spread peanut butter on one slice of bread.

2 Spread some jam on the peanut butter.

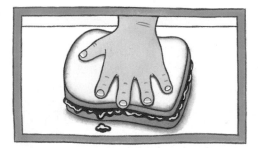

3 Place another slice of bread on top.

4 Cut the bread into sandwiches and eat!

Copy and complete these sentences.
When you make a peanut __1__ and __2__ sandwich
you need two slices of __3__ . You need a __4__ to
cut the bread into sandwiches. You also need a
jar of __5__ butter and a __6__ of jam to spread on
the bread.

Thinking about it

Answer each question with a sensible sentence.
1 What do you need to make a peanut butter
   and jam sandwich?
2 What is the first thing you do?
3 What do you do after this?
4 What is the third thing you do?
5 What is the last thing you do?

Thinking it through

1 What is your favourite type of sandwich?
2 Write some instructions for making your
   favourite sandwich.
3 Make a list of some important things to
   remember in the kitchen. Do it like this:

Things to remember in the kitchen

• Always wash your hands.

UNIT 6 Granny Granny, please comb my Hair

Think ahead

Look at the title of the poem.
What do you think it is going to be about?

Granny Granny
please comb my hair
you always take your time
you always take such care

You put me to sit down on a cushion
between your knees
you rub a little coconut oil
parting gentle as a breeze
Mummy Mummy
she's always in a hurry-hurry
rush
she pulls my hair
sometimes she tugs

But Granny
you have all the time in the world
and when you're finished
you always turn my head and
say
'Now who's a nice girl.'

From *That Stuff* by Grace Nichols

Choose the best ending for each sentence.
1 The girl wants Granny to
  a) read her a story b) comb her hair
2 Granny sits the girl
  a) on a cushion b) on her lap
3 Granny always takes a lot of
  a) coconut oil   b) care
4 The girl's Mum is always
  a) in a mood   b) in a rush

Thinking about it

Write sensible answers to each question.
1 Name three things the girl likes when Granny combs her hair.
2 Why doesn't the girl like her Mum to comb her hair?
3 Why do you think her Mum is always in a rush?

Thinking it through

1 How can you tell Granny loves the little girl?
2 How can you tell the little girl loves her Granny?
3 What other things do you think the girl and her Granny might do together?

UNIT 7 Willy and Hugh

Think ahead

What sort of animal do you think Hugh is?

Willy was lonely. Everyone seemed to have friends. Everyone except Willy. No one let him join in any games; they all said he was useless. One day Willy was walking in the park, minding his own business, and Hugh Jape was running ... they met.

They sat down on a bench and watched the joggers. 'Looks like they're really enjoying themselves,' said Hugh. Willy laughed.

Buster Nose appeared. 'I've been looking for you, little wimp,' he sneered.

Hugh stood up. 'Can I be of any help?' he asked. Buster left. Very quickly.

Then they went to the library and Willy read to Hugh. As they were leaving the library, Hugh stopped suddenly ... He'd seen a TERRIFYING CREATURE ...

'Can I be of any help?' asked Willy, and he carefully moved the spider out of the way.

'Shall we meet up again tomorrow?' asked Hugh.

'Yes, that would be great,' said Willy.

From *Willy and Hugh* by Anthony Browne

> *Thinking back*

Copy these sentences. Fill in the gaps with sensible words.

Willy had no __1__ . No-one let him join in any of their __2__ . One day Willy met Hugh Jape in the __3__ . They sat down on a __4__ and watched the joggers. When they were in the __5__ Hugh Jape was __6__ by a spider. Willy __7__ the spider. __8__ and Hugh Jape became good friends.

> *Thinking about it*

Write a sensible sentence to answer each question.
1 How were people unkind to Willy?
2 How did Willy and Hugh meet?
3 How do you know Buster Nose was a bully?
4 How did Hugh help Willy in the park?
5 How did Willy help Hugh in the library?

> *Thinking it through*

1 How do you think Willy felt at the beginning of the story? Say why.
2 How do you think Willy felt at the end of the story? Say why.
3 What makes a good friend? Make a list of some things.

UNIT 8   The Hare and the Tortoise

Think ahead

Which can run faster – a hare or a tortoise?
If they had a race, who would win?

Hare was always boasting because he could run fast. One day he was bored. He decided to have some fun, so he asked Tortoise to give him a race.

1 Hare ran very fast. Tortoise could only walk slowly. Hare was soon a long way ahead.

2 Hare decided there was no need to rush so he had a sleep.

3 Tortoise just kept plodding on. In a while he passed Hare, who was still sleeping.

4 When Hare woke up it was too late! Tortoise was at the finishing line. Hare had lost the race.

Thinking back

Match up the beginnings and endings of these sentences. Write the complete sentences in your book.

1 Hare boasted because   won the race.
2 Tortoise could only   have a sleep.
3 Hare decided to   he could run fast.
4 Tortoise passed Hare and   walk slowly.

Thinking about it

Write a sensible answer to each question.
1 Why did Hare ask Tortoise for a race?
2 Do you think it was a fair race? Say why.
3 Would you say Hare was a show-off? Why?
4 Do you think Hare was upset when he lost?

Thinking it through

1 The story has a moral. It teaches us a lesson.
Which of these does it teach:
a) It is good to be a fast runner.
b) Don't give up. Always keep trying.
2 Hare was fast but Tortoise was slow.
Write the opposites of these words:
a) hot   b) asleep   c) hard   d) heavy   e) win
3 Find out and write what the word 'perseverance' means. In the story, who had perseverance?

UNIT 9   About Books

Think ahead
How many different sorts of books can you think of?

This is an
information book
(non-fiction)

This is a story book
(fiction)

Titles

All about
insects

*The Big
Adventure*
By Margaret Jones

By Ruby Clarke
Illustrated by Maria Gowland

Illustrated by Roger Stevens

Authors (people who
wrote the books)

Illustrators (people who drew the pictures)

➤ Thinking back

Complete each sentence correctly.

1 The title of the story book is

_____ .

2 The title of the information book is

_____ .

3 Ruby Clarke wrote _____,_____ .

4 Roger Stevens illustrated _____ .

➤ Thinking about it

Answer each question with a sentence.

1 What is an author?

2 What is an illustrator?

3 Why do you think illustrators are important?

4 Why are book titles important?

5 What is a non-fiction book?

6 Is a story book a fiction or non-fiction book?

➤ Thinking it through

1 Write the title of a good fiction book you have read. Name the author and the illustrator of it.

2 Write the title of an information book you have used recently. What was it about?

3 An encyclopaedia is a non-fiction book. Explain what an encyclopaedia is.

4 What is a dictionary used for? Is it a fiction or non-fiction book?

UNIT 10 Bedtime

Think ahead

Do you ever try to stay up later than your bedtime?
What reasons do you give?

Five minutes, five minutes more, please!
Let me just stay five minutes more!

Can't I just finish the castle
I'm building here on the floor?

Can't I just finish the story
I'm reading here in my book?

Can't I just finish this bead chain –
It almost is finished, look!

Can't I just finish this game, please?
When a game's once begun
It's a pity never to find out
Whether you've lost or won.

Can't I just stay five minutes?
Well, can't I just stay four?

Three minutes, then? two minutes?
Can't I stay one minute more?

From *Bedtime* by Eleanor Farjeon

➤ *Thinking back*

Choose the best ending for each sentence.
1 On the floor, the child was building a
   a) tower   b) garage   c) castle
2 The child was reading
   a) a book   b) a comic   c) a magazine
3 The child was making
   a) a daisy chain   b) a bicycle chain
   c) a bead chain
4 The child had just started playing a
   a) game   b) tape   c) video

➤ *Thinking about it*

1 What reason did the child give for wanting to finish the game?
2 Who do you think the child was talking to?
3 Do you think the child asked to stay up late often? sometimes? rarely? Give a reason for your answer.

➤ *Thinking it through*

1 Which words have a similar meaning to 'asking'?
   watching   requesting   playing   begging
2 What excuses do you give for wanting to stay up late?
3 What reasons do parents give for going to bed at a certain time?

UNIT 11 Face to Face with a Dragon

Think ahead

Do you think the dragon in this story will be a real dragon or not?

The Chinese celebrate their New Year with colourful procations and festivals. Often people dress up as dragons and dance through the streets.

Chin Chiang pulled her by the hand, and they hurried down the stairs together – round and round, down, down, down, to the market street. The sound of firecrackers exploded in their ears while the eager crowd buzzed and hummed. Chin Chiang pushed his way forward, but Pu Yee pulled back. In the noise and confusion Chin Chiang let go of her hand, and suddenly he came face to face with the dragon whose head was wreathed in smoke.

From *Chin Chiang and the Dragon Dance* by Ian Wallace

➤ *Thinking back*

Think of a suitable word to complete each sentence.

1 Chin Chiang and Pu Yee went down the
 _____ together.
2 Chin Chiang and Pu Yee went down to the
 _____ street.
3 They heard the sound of _____ exploding.
4 Chin Chiang let go of Pu Yee's _____ .
5 Chin Chiang came face to face with a _____ .

➤ *Thinking about it*

Answer these with sensible sentences.

1 Name some things Chinese people do to
 celebrate their New Year.
2 Was Chin Chiang a boy or a girl?
3 Did Chin Chiang live downstairs or upstairs?
4 What do you think might happen next?

➤ *Thinking it through*

1 What do you think 'the eager crowd buzzed
 and hummed' really means?
2 Describe how you think the dragon looked.
3 How do you think Chin Chiang felt when he
 came face to face with the dragon? Why?

Contents and Index Pages

Think ahead

The contents page and index below come from a book, called Things at Home. *What sort of things would you expect to find in it?*

Many books have a contents page and an index. The contents page tells you how the book is organised. The index tells you where to find things.

Contents

Index

Thinking back

Where would you find information on:
1 Washing Machines   2 Television
3 Watches and Clocks   4 Telephones
5 Vacuum Cleaners?

Thinking about it

Where do you think you might find some information on:
1 cereals   2 chairs   3 drains
4 electricity 5 aerials?

Thinking it through

1 Why do some books have a contents page?
2 Look in the library. Write the name of a fiction and non-fiction book that each has a contents page.
3 Where would you find an index page in a book?
4 Explain the difference between an index and a contents page.
5 Which page is organised in alphabetical order? Why do you think this is?
6 Can you think of any books that are organised in alphabetical order?

UNIT 13 The Blind Men and the Elephant

Think ahead

How would you describe an elephant?

One day someone bought an elephant to a village where six blind men lived.

The first blind man touched the elephant. He felt its trunk. 'An elephant is like a snake,' he said. 'It is long and rubbery.'

The second man felt its tusks. 'It's like a sharp knife,' he said.

The third man felt its ear. 'It's like a leaf, big and smooth.'

The fourth man felt its leg. 'It's like a tree. It's round and hard,' he said.

The fifth man felt the side of the elephant. 'It's just like a wall,' he said. 'It's high and wide.'

Lastly, the sixth man felt its tail. 'It's like a long, thin rope.'

After they had all touched the elephant, they began to argue. Each blind man thought he was right. In a way, they were *all* partly right.

Thinking back

Write a sentence about each blind man. Say what part of the elephant each man touched.

Thinking about it

Write sensible sentences to answer these questions.

1 How do you know the men could not see? What clues are there?
2 Why did each man think the elephant was something different?
3 Why did the blind men all argue with each other?
4 What does it mean when it says, 'In a way, they were *all* partly right'?

Thinking it through

1 Write some sentences and say what you think happened after the story. What did the men say to each other? What did they tell their friends about their experiences?
2 What do you think we can learn from the story?
3 Imagine the blind men touched a crocodile for the first time. Write some of the things they might say.

UNIT 14 From a Tadpole to a Frog

Think ahead

Look at the pictures. How do frogs begin their lives?

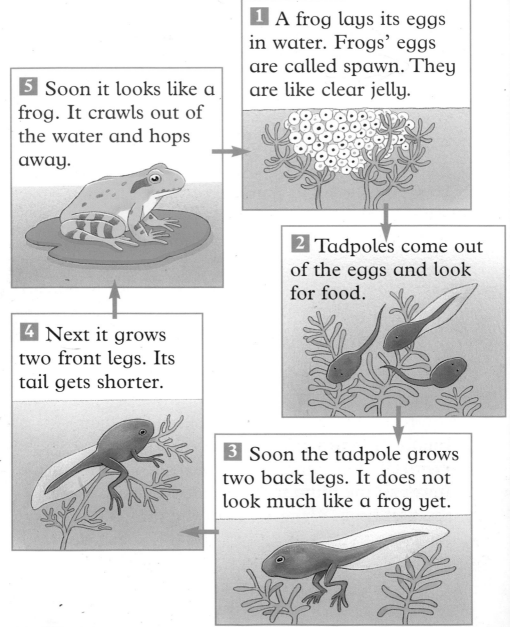

1 A frog lays its eggs in water. Frogs' eggs are called spawn. They are like clear jelly.

5 Soon it looks like a frog. It crawls out of the water and hops away.

2 Tadpoles come out of the eggs and look for food.

4 Next it grows two front legs. Its tail gets shorter.

3 Soon the tadpole grows two back legs. It does not look much like a frog yet.

30

Thinking back

Choose the correct words to complete the sentences.
1 A frog lays its eggs (on land, in water).
2 Frogs' eggs are called (spawn, jelly).
3 Out of the eggs come (butterflies, tadpoles).
4 Each tadpole grows two back (legs, teeth).
5 The tadpole's tail gets (longer, shorter).
6 Tadpoles turn into (frogs, fish).

Thinking about it

These sentences are in a muddle.
Write them in their correct order.
Then each tadpole grows two back legs.
First the frog lays its eggs.
When it becomes a frog it comes out of the water.
After this it grows two front legs.
Next the tadpoles come out of the eggs.

Thinking it through

1 Find out, and write, what the word 'hatch' means.
2 In what ways is a tadpole similar to a caterpillar?
3 People often say frogs are ugly. Do you agree or disagree? Say why.

UNIT 15 A Dark, Dark Tale

Think ahead

Look at the pictures. Do you think the story takes place at night time or in the day?

Once upon a time there was a dark, dark moor.
On the moor there was a dark, dark wood.

In the wood there was a dark, dark house.
At the front of the house there was a dark, dark door.

Behind the door there was a dark, dark hall.
In the hall there were some dark, dark stairs.

Up the stairs there was a dark, dark passage.
Across the passage there was a dark, dark curtain.

Behind the curtain there was a dark, dark room.
In the room there was a dark, dark cupboard.

In the cupboard there was a dark, dark corner.
In the corner was a dark, dark box.

And in the box there was ...
A MOUSE!

From *A Dark, Dark Tale* by Ruth Brown

➡ *Thinking back*

Copy these sentences and think of a sensible ending for them.

1 On the dark, dark moor there was a _____ .
2 In the dark, dark wood there was a _____ .
3 In the dark, dark hall there were some _____ .
4 In the corner there was a dark, dark _____ .
5 In the box there was a _____ .

➡ *Thinking about it*

1 The story starts on a dark, dark moor. Write it backwards, starting from the mouse. Do it like this:

> The mouse was in a dark, dark box.
> The box was in a dark, dark corner.
> The corner was _____ .

➡ *Thinking it through*

1 Make up a different ending. Think of something else you might have found in the box.
2 How does the author make the story feel a bit scary?
3 Write some things you don't like when it's dark.

UNIT 16 Mr Cosmo the Conjuror

Think ahead
What sort of things does a conjuror do?

It was early morning. There was excitement in town.
As if by magic, posters had appeared.
They said: MR COSMO IS COMING!
'Mr Cosmo is coming!' everybody
said. 'Mr Cosmo is coming!'
'Who is Mr Cosmo?'

On a hill outside the town, a
caravan appeared. A horse
was pulling it, a performing
dog was chasing it, six
pigeons were flying over it, six
rabbits were peering out of it,
and *nobody* was driving it!

The caravan entered the
town. Everybody followed.
The caravan stopped.
Everybody gathered
round. The caravan
door opened.
Everybody stared.
There in the
doorway stood a
man, a woman, a
boy and a girl.

From *Mr Cosmo the Conjuror* by
Allan Ahlberg and Joe Wright

Thinking back

Write a sentence to answer each question.
1 Who was coming to town?
2 What appeared on the hill, outside the town?
3 What was the horse doing?
4 Who appeared in the doorway of the caravan?

Thinking about it

Now write sentences to answer these questions.
1 Why was everyone in town excited?
2 What surprised people when they saw the caravan?
3 What job do you think Mr Cosmo did?
4 Who do you think the man, woman and children were at the end?

Thinking it through

Think of some good answers for these questions.
1 How could the posters have appeared in town 'as if by magic'?
2 Was it really true that there was no-one driving the caravan? Say why.
3 Write three sentences about what you think happened next.
4 Write about something you have seen that made you very excited.

UNIT 17 Neigh, Cluck, Quack and Tweet

Think ahead
What sort of animals would you expect to see on a farm? What noises would they make?

Neigh, neigh chestnut horse,
Mane and tail fly.
Gallop, gallop to the gate,
Tuck your hooves up high.

Cluck busy speckled hen,
Cluck, cluck, scratch.
Hurry, hurry to your nest,
Will the eggs hatch?

Quack yellow mother duck,
Quack for your brood.
Quick, quack over here,
Lots of lovely food.

Tweet, tweet, chirpy bird,
Singing in your tree.
Look out from the topmost branch,
Tell me what you see.

From *First Rhymes* by Lucy Coats

Thinking back

Write a sentence to answer each question.
1 Which animal clucked?
2 Which animal made a tweeting noise?
3 Which animal neighed?
4 Which animal quacked?

Thinking about it

Now write sentences to answer these questions.
1 What parts of the horse's body are mentioned?
2 Has the hen got any chicks yet?
3 What word is used for the duck's family?
4 Where is the bird singing?

Thinking it through

Think of some good answers for these questions.
1 Write a word that rhymes with:
  a) fly   b) scratch   c) brood   d) tree
2 What word is used when a horse runs fast?
3 What other animals might there have been on the farm?
4 Think of a way to finish this verse:
    Moo sleepy brown cow,
    Moo at the gate.
    Will the farmer milk you
    _____ ?

Think ahead

Look at the poster. What sort of farm do you think Valley Farm is?

Valley Farm
A real working farm

* Horses, goats, sheep, cows, pigs, chickens, ducks
* Museum of old farm machinery
* Picnic tables and lunch rooms
* Café for refreshments
* Gift shop
* Free parking
* Schools welcome
* Near the motorway
* Open 7 days a week

Thinking back

Write and say if these sentences are true or false.

1 The name of the farm is Vale Farm.
2 There are lots of different animals on the farm.
3 There is a museum of old farm machinery.
4 You have to pay for parking.
5 It is possible to visit the farm on a Saturday.

Thinking about it

Write sensible sentences to answer these questions.

1 Where could you eat your lunch if it was wet?
2 Where could you buy something to eat?
3 Where could you buy a present to take home?
4 Is Valley Farm easy to reach by car? How can you tell?
5 Could you visit the farm on a school trip?

Thinking it through

1 Write some sentences about some things you might enjoy seeing and doing at the farm. Write about some things you might not enjoy (like the mud and the smell, for example!)
2 List some jobs that have to be done at the farm.
3 In your book, write the names of some animals' babies, such as horse – foal.

UNIT 19 Animal Homes

Think ahead
Why does everyone need a home?
Do you know the names of any animal homes?

Rabbits live in tunnels underground. These are called **burrows**. In their burrows they are safe and warm away from their enemies.

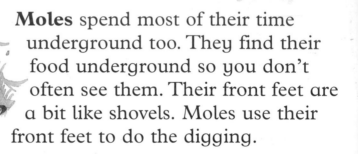

Moles spend most of their time underground too. They find their food underground so you don't often see them. Their front feet are a bit like shovels. Moles use their front feet to do the digging.

Hedgehogs sometimes live in old rabbit burrows but often they will just roll up in a pile of old leaves. At night they go looking for worms and slugs.

Badgers also dig lots of tunnels and have a home underground. These tunnels lead to its home called an **earth** or a **sett**. Badgers stay in their sett until night time. Then it will come out and look for food.

Thinking back

Write each sentence with the correct ending.

1 Rabbits live in tunnels called (dens, setts, burrows)
2 Moles have feet like (forks, shovels, knives)
3 Moles use their feet to (dig, eat, fight)
4 Hedgehogs eat (wood, worms, wool)
5 Badgers live (in trees, in the water, underground)

Thinking about it

Answer these questions with sensible sentences.

1 Why do rabbits live underground?
2 Why aren't moles seen very often?
3 What do hedgehogs use piles of old leaves for?
4 In what way are badgers like moles?

Thinking it through

1 Who do you think the enemies of rabbits are?
2 Some people believe that badgers and moles have poor eyesight. Why do you think that might be?
3 Some people have built themselves homes underground. Think of three advantages and three disadvantages of living underground.

UNIT 20 Pooh Bear Gets Stuck

Think ahead

Have you ever read any other Winnie the Pooh stories? What sort of animal is Winnie the Pooh?

Pooh went to visit Rabbit down his hole and got stuck.

'Hello, are you stuck?' Rabbit asked.

'N-no,' said Pooh carelessly. 'Just resting and thinking and humming to myself.'

'Here, give us a paw.'

Pooh stretched out a paw, and Rabbit pulled and pulled and pulled ...

'*Ow!*' cried Pooh. 'You're hurting!'

'The fact is,' said Rabbit, 'you're stuck.'

'It all comes,' said Pooh crossly, 'of not having front doors big enough.'

'It all comes,' said Rabbit sternly, 'of eating too much ... I shall just have to go and fetch Christopher Robin.'

Christopher Robin lived at the other end of the Forest, and when he came back with Rabbit, and saw the front half of Pooh, he said, 'Silly old Bear,' in such a loving voice that everybody felt quite hopeful again.

From *Winnie the Pooh* by AA Milne

Thinking back

Write if each sentence is true or false.
1 Pooh went to visit Rabbit.
2 Rabbit got stuck.
3 Rabbit tried to pull Pooh out.
4 Rabbit went to fetch Christopher Robin.
5 Christopher Robin lived in the village.

Thinking about it

Write sensible answers to these questions.
1 When Pooh got stuck, what did he blame it on?
2 What did Rabbit blame it on?
3 Why do you think Rabbit could not pull Pooh out?
4 How do you know Pooh was coming out of the hole head first?

Thinking it through

1 How do you think:
   a) Rabbit felt when he saw that Pooh was stuck?
   b) Pooh felt when he got stuck?
   c) Christopher Robin felt when he saw Pooh stuck?
2 How can you tell Christopher Robin liked Pooh?
3 Think of some ways of getting Pooh unstuck. Write them in your book.

UNIT 21 Our Family Comes From Around the World

Think ahead
What do you think the title of the poem means?

Our family comes
From around the world:
Our hair is straight,
Our hair is curled,
Our eyes are brown,
Our eyes are blue,
Our skins are different
Colours, too.

We're girls and boys,
We're big and small,
We're young and old,
We're short and tall.
We're everything
That we can be
And still we are
A family.

We laugh and cry,
We work and play,
We help each other
Every day.
The world's a lovely
Place to be
Because we are
A family.

From *Fathers, Mothers, Sisters,*
Brothers by Mary Ann Hoberman

➤ *Thinking back*

Match up each sentence with one that means the opposite. Write the pairs of sentences in your book.

1 Our hair is straight.   We're small.
2 We're girls.   We're old.
3 We're big.   Our hair is curled.
4 We're young.   We cry.
5 We laugh.   We're boys.

➤ *Thinking about it*

Name five ways in which the poem says everyone is different. Do it like this:

> 1 We have different hair styles.
> 2 We have different colour eyes.

➤ *Thinking it through*

1 Did you like the poem? Give your reasons.
2 Which sentences tell you what the poem is about.
   It is no fun to be in a family.
   We are all different in some ways.
   We all belong to one big family.
3 In what way is your school a family?
4 Write some things we could do to make the world a better place.

UNIT 22 The Winter Hedgehog

Think ahead

Why do you think hedgehogs sleep for most of the winter?

One cold, misty autumn afternoon, the hedgehogs gathered in a wood. They were searching the undergrowth for leaves for their nests, preparing for the long sleep of winter. All, that is, except one.

The smallest hedgehog had overheard two foxes talking about winter. 'What is winter?' he had asked his mother.

'Winter comes when we are asleep,' she had replied. 'It can be very beautiful, but it can also be dangerous, cruel and very, very cold. It's not for the likes of us. Now go to sleep.'

But the smallest hedgehog couldn't sleep. As evening fell he slipped away to look for winter. When hedgehogs are determined they can move very swiftly, and soon the little hedgehog was far from home. An owl swooped down from high in a tree. 'Hurry home,' he called. 'It's time for your long sleep.' But on and on went the smallest hedgehog until the sky turned dark and the trees were nothing but shadows.

From *The Winter Hedgehog* by Ann and Roger Cartwright

➡ *Thinking back*

Choose the correct answer to each question.
1 Where did the hedgehogs gather?
   a) in the forest   b) in the park   c) in a wood
2 What were they searching for?
   a) leaves   b) food   c) their way home
3 What did the smallest hedgehog go looking for?
   a) his mother   b) winter   c) a friend

➡ *Thinking about it*

Answer these questions with sensible sentences.
1 How did the hedgehog's mother describe winter?
2 Why couldn't the smallest hedgehog sleep?
3 Where do you think he slept that night?
4 What was the weather like the next morning?

➡ *Thinking it through*

1 Which of these words do you think describes
  the smallest hedgehog?
  determined   sleepy   prickly   brave
  adventurous   foolish   slow   curious
2 How do you think the hedgehog's mother felt
  when she found her son missing? What would
  she have said and done?
3 What dangers might the small hedgehog face
  on his own?